VELLUM

Vellum

MATT DONOVAN

A MARINER ORIGINAL

Houghton Mifflin Company   Boston   New York

2007

Library of Congress Cataloging-in-Publication Data
Donovan, Matt.
Vellum / Matt Donovan.
p.   cm.
ISBN-13: 978-0-618-82212-6
ISBN-10: 0-618-82212-7
I. Title.
PS3604.05673V35 2007
813'.6 — dc22   2006031328

Book design by Melissa Lotfy

Printed in the United States of America

MP 10 9 8 7 6 5 4 3 2 1

for my parents
and
for Ligia

CONTENTS

Part III

"There are no limits to our verbs, our forms," Matt Donovan writes in "*Saint Catherine in an O:* A Song About Knives,"

> think of the knife
> that slits an orange or bundled iris stems, the one strapped
> to the rooster's varnished spur. The dagger, poniard, dirk.
>
> Edge that snips the line . . .

Donovan's poem is concerned with the inescapable ambiguity of any tool. A knife "whittles an owl, juliennes" and, in Sudan, becomes the horrifying instrument by means of which the hopeful will no longer be allowed to "hold the future." A knife sliding on steel guitar strings whines out a particular song; a blade cuts grain for the harvest or randomly slashes the nests of swallows. Are swords beaten into ploughshares, or are ploughshares hammered into weapons? Both, of course, and this terrifying ambiguity at the core of human making is Donovan's inescapable subject. To make a sheet of vellum, the parchment page on which the beautiful martyrdom of a saint will be represented in dazzling perfection, an animal is

> bled & flayed & turned, as was always its purpose,
> into the page of this psalm.

You can't embrace the world of art without acknowledging the horrible uses to which our arts are put, as a poem like "Montezuma's Painters" makes startlingly clear. For the Aztec artists sent to record the appearance of the strangers on their shore, the new arrivals are marvelously clad and equipped; what are these unknown objects that accompany them, these spectacular works of artifice? In the paintings they produce for their curious emperor,

> Each thing seemed just as it should:
> each particular was beautifully faithful to itself,
>
> . . . & their uses still unimaginable.

In the twenty-first century it is no longer possible for the destructive use of any tool to be unimaginable; we have every reason to believe that anything that can be turned toward destruction will be. We wish that there were "limits to our verbs" at the same time as we seek to deny any limitation to human making. To create anything, Donovan seems to suggest, even a Sistine ceiling, is to destroy something else. The knife that carves is the knife that flays. To be human is to reside in the landscape of damage and to make from the wreck of things our accomplishments, even as we leave more wreckage in our paths.

It isn't Donovan's work to catalogue his damages in any autobiographical sense. The speaker we meet here comes with little biography attached, but with a sensibility firmly in place. Donovan's "I" is recorder, questioner, meditator, aesthetic philosopher, wondering citizen. His way of "holding the future" — such as it is — lies in the persistence of the will to make beautiful gestures of ordering in the face of the cruelties his poems witness. At least he can point to the way the water spills and pours from Bernini's fountain with a sound that seems to mean both "abundance" and "drowning" at once, one no less real than the other. The signature of this speaker's character is his obsession with the deeply ambiguous thing any act of making is.

Including the making of poems. *Vellum,* of course, suggests that these are also pages, also acts of illumination, and that the poems themselves are grounded in a kind of slaughter, or at least in the knowledge of damage and of loss. The knife "snips the line." Writing on paper, even on a computer screen, Donovan inscribes upon something that has been destroyed and transformed another act of creation. The sure grace of Donovan's syntax, the authority of his descriptive gestures, the exacting shaping of stanza — all firmly ally him with the artists who people his pages, from Botticelli to Charlie Chaplin, Zeuxis to Severn, Houdini to Neruda.

Thus the paradox in which this poet traffics is that these chronicles of the terrifying contradictions in all our human projects are themselves marvelously well made. This points us all the more toward the darkly alluring fusion of beauty and ruthlessness at the core of art. It's rare to encounter a first book lit by such a developed vision of the nature of things. Donovan's is a serious, companionable poetry, and his book — as the best art does — harrows and consoles at once, and gives to one impulse no more power than the other. In this way it mirrors, brilliantly, something of how it is to live.

MARK DOTY

Nobody should wonder that wood
for funeral pyres is painted.

—PLINY THE ELDER,
Historia Naturalis

Part I

Pulling Down the Sky

(the Sistine Chapel)

Piece by piece the sky was hacked, the star-flung heaven made years before,

its sheen of gold & ultramarine. And the firmament turned to pigmented dust

that caked & stained their forearms & necks & rained down in wide, benedictory arcs

into the space below. It grew dark, of course, & they worked torch-lit

& a man said *plaster, bucket.* A man said *scaffold, whore.* And the hammers

mauling the sky from that height swallowed up the sounds from below:

a robed boy scurrying from the candles, the sunset vesper thrum.

And when they rested, they saw the ruin they had made & knew what was needed

would be done. To pull down the entire barrel vault blue, each starred width

of heaven. To prepare the space where the sky had been for, yes, a god

& the shapes of god. Of cloth, a mule, a knuckle. An axe, a bowl, some bread.

Saint Catherine in an O: A Song About Knives

On a page of vellum — *Saint Catherine in an O* — within
a letter made of vine-sprawl, imbricate bulbs, & the scarlet
interlaced whorl of petal cupping calyx cupping stem, a woman

offers her neck. It's a kind of ready-made scene — the saint kneeling
on a cropped wedge of earth, someone with a crown in a tower,
& a swordsman who is only a frocked booted boy pulling back

his robe for his work — & seems carelessly done, as if the illuminator
chose death to be a kind of afterthought to vermilion. To leaf-curl,
areola, awl-shaped stems, his blossoms' dazzling tangle. As if

this were response enough. *O, omphalos.* Meaning *center* & *navel,*
meaning the first time a blade touches flesh. And meaning here
a frame of plenitude through which we witness again.

There are no limits to our verbs, our forms:
                                        think of the knife
that slits an orange or bundled iris stems, the one strapped
to the rooster's varnished spur. The dagger, poniard, dirk.

Edge that snips the line, whittles an owl, juliennes, traces a lip.
A cut, an incision, a gouge. In Sudan, the story goes, when the slogan
of reform was *The Future's in Your Hands,* men scavenged the streets

waving machetes, hacking off hands above the wrist, asking
How will you hold the future now? The stiletto, the skean, the scythe.
The choosing, the mark, the tool. Beneath a concrete bridge,

shirtless & drunk, a boy works his way through the swallows' nests,
slashing until each mud cone-shape drops into the river, dissolves.
Yet to say so is hardly enough. To say *pigsticker, bayonet, shiv.*

Because in Waco, behind Benny's Gas & Go, a man plays slide guitar
with his pocketknife, accompanying the words of his songs —
one about light, the Lord moving on water, about what will be

by & by; how blood, he knows, will make him whole, & blades
that changed into doves.
                                        Or because this splendor of color ends
on the parchment in a burnished gold resembling a cluster of burrs,

the kind of thing that would have snagged in a cow's mottled hide
as it grazed on grass tufts or slogged its way home. Staring, bewildered
in the stillness, it may survive this way for a few days more

before it is bled & flayed & turned, as was always its purpose,
into the page of this psalm. Here, near the margin, are traces of it still:
patterns of skin, a texture like velvet, follicles, the throat's scalloped curve.

Montezuma's Painters

Fly swats & muddied cloaks, slop buckets
& greyhound tongues.

> *From behind the grasses they watched*
> *& on bark paper strips & henequen cloth*
> *rendered what they saw.*

Torn linen bandaging a thigh. And their black beards,
their anchored ships, the wooden crates of quail.

> *For this is what he had asked.*

Buckles, cups made of Florentine glass, hides
stitched into wine-heavy sacks.

> *And while some carried*
> *maize cakes, baked fish, & plums,*
> *the images were rushed back, inland, to him*

Crossbows, the cannons' inlaid brass, tattered pennants,
each length of pearls.

> *so that he too might see these men & the shapes*
> *of all they had brought.*

Their crimson caps, muskets, hammered bronze,
tassels, scabbards, & blades.

> *Each thing seemed just as it should:*
> *each particular was beautifully faithful to itself,*
> *the details were lavish, exact,*

Half-greaves & back plates catching midday sun,
ash-colored horse tethered to a palm —

& their uses still unimaginable.

Small Blessing for a Child

Where to begin with what you've never seen? Lemon-throated finches

scuffling the Russian olive? How one path's pollen-heavy heaps of chamisa
lead to a stippled bit of scrap metal inscribing some loved thing's grave?
What, of the endless, sad cache of beauty, will you pitch towards, too?

Nectarine snared in the half-moon's burn, the way this winter sun refracts
from the birdbath to the garden wall & engraves a fleeting shimmer.
Our not-yet, nameless one still at the threshold of this world,

what good can it do for me to describe some one-off pause of mine? Lost
beneath a city years ago, mapless, anonymous, I heard a man bang out
Amazing Grace with a mallet on a saw: in fluorescent light shafting

tiled subway walls, fixed before the exact, useless work of hands
flitting at steel, I found a shrill, wavering *Amen.* May you find, too,
a scarce *so-it-is,* but let it be of your own making. May what crams the air

be your precise hammering, your erratic, stumbled-into song.

Fumbling with a Field Guide on the Back Arroyo Trail

I write *ash* in my notebook & think less of leaf-shape or branches
below me on the ridge than of acoustics, monosyllabics,
the need to evoke what remains, even if none of it corresponds
to this morning's lit particulars: sage clumps & clustered indigo petals,

juniper & yucca blooms. Or what I'm guessing is *cottonwood* now.
I can name so little of this world & have been trying, hopelessly,
with a field guide again, to affix nouns to what's within reach. For now
it's even all I ask. To unfold my pocketknife, cut a single blade of grass,

to walk deeper into this silence & have it fill with words. Years ago,
during a performance at a church, I heard *4'33"*,
a piece composed of nothing but silence that seemed to be only
a joke. The pianist bowed ceremoniously, then sat motionless,

poised, his fingers merely resting on the keys. A cough, mints
eased from cellophane. A snicker. Some wind-flung dirt.
And then the sounds from a practice room below rising up
through the floor: the opening notes of the *Moonlight* Sonata,

barely recognizable, barely played at all, hands cascading
in a bungling forte that lurched the melody a little further along
before the chords collapsed & whoever was playing pummeled the keys
& bellowed *For Christ's sake! Shit!* & began again. Which made

the silence bearable. Which made the silence his & filled the room
with inaccuracies that gave us a reason for praise. Were it not
for these raven wings quickening the air, or the riverbed trickle
from yesterday's storm when flash floods washed out whole roads,

this moment might approach silence too. This is only another walk
in which I try to learn words for whatever's in my hand, in which
I'll skim drawings of quackgrass & sprangletop & six bluestems
& recognize none of it & give up this gray-blue bit of scrub

&, despite today what I'd promised & planned, thread down the path
a few miles more where it dead-ends in a field of shot-up cars.
There, at least, amid the metal's ruin & a sea of broken glass,
are the wild, indelible loops of graffiti, the retrievable,

effortless names: *Oz Sucks Dick. Popper on the Loose. Dibz.*
The Good Son. Sack D. Many miles from here, trying to waste
an afternoon, I once found a deer collapsed near a lake — sleek,
immaculate, & unmoving except for its antlers, which swarmed

with orange-&-black-speckled butterflies that obliterated
the velvet beneath. Whatever word explains this,
I don't want to know it yet. I only watched them open & fold
sporadically, or in what looked like unison at times,

& when even more flickered across the grasses & collected on its rack,
the deer became, because of their gathering, something else
entirely, & the insects became, too, as soundless & implausible
as the accents & breves that once covered a man's book while he watched

from across a café. This is, at least, how it's told. In Berkeley, in exile,
he glimpses a woman working, pen in hand, through a book of poems
he recognizes as his own. She seems almost frantic, scribbling
annotations & scanning each syllable, oblivious of the crowd

& plate-clatter around her, darkening everything she reads.
When finally he rises, & stands behind her, & watches her hand
now quicken across an elegy for his cousin, he sees the words,
as he put it, *devoured.* And knew then what he'd written — *smoke,*

a pair of trousers, quicklime, & clover — was all wrong & would never last.

Charlie Chaplin Dug Up & Ransomed: A Prayer

That my body, Lord, might rise too, resurrected reluctantly from earth,
given the rainwater, the dawn begun, grave walls pitched into ooze,

given that the scheme to bury me deeper in my own grave's dirt will fail
because of schnapps & mud & Lord, let the breath of those who deliver me

that night be sweetened by cherry-tipped cigars. Allow what will lift me
fumbling the first March of my death to be not only a shovel, the grace of rope,

a mechanic's coat trussed to brass handles, but also the plan for a paid-for garage,
paved cement floors, a procession of wrenches in a drawer. Grant me

morning light in a pickup bed, lying within earshot of Bulgarian songs that rhyme
thigh with *smoke* & permit me, Lord, once hangovers wane, to be stashed

at the far edge of a field, close to the rocks of a fishing spot where a thief will always —
or for more than a week — watch me, conceal me, keep me in spring heat, devour

a plum & suck its pit clean, dream of cash he half knows won't come. Let my reward,
Lord, be crow wings, furrows, bits of last year's stalks, three threadbare burlap sacks.

Second Pilgrimage, Rodeo Nites

Plastic bags webbing the hedges. Vent steam tumbling, becoming

sky. Snow-heaped semis & this gang-tagged wall, choral whine
of Route 25. So it's not that there's somehow nothing now,
although two weeks back, breaking from tequilas & the El Ray Dukes,

in this back lot between Rodeo Nites & the Cactus Lodge Motel
with a tottering group from the bar, I stood here, staring up
into the darkness of a pine, our waitress slurring *Do you see them?*

again, her flashlight's meager beam threading the limbs until,
at last, we could see: the teeming, shadow alive with shadow, bats
writhing every inch of the tree. Amid the zoo-scent & skittering

— what we were brought here for — parsing wing-flutter
from the wind's branch sway, trying to glimpse each portion
of darkness before it winged into night, we were all transfixed,

stock-still & knowing — what? Nothing, I think, beyond the moment's
sheer improbable fact, the out-of-nowhere, inscrutable *this*
in which we're dazzled by a shivering thing. Some mornings,

what I feel is almost envy for anything resembling faith's grip.
Is that what I mean to say? Knowing something moves each
extinguishable star, the on-side fourth-quarter kick? Not quite.

We know Botticelli heaped his secular work upon Savonarola's flames.
Without much, we guess, regret. Without watching — here I'll guess, too —
how a beak-nosed man whose palms did not cup light changed

in an instant to ash. Each for-its-own-sake olive sprig, plume,
gauzed matter-of-fact ringlet curl — those rendered bits of grace
that might otherwise have lasted, gone in that impetuous blaze.

I know this is hopeless now: there's no sign of the ceaseless
scuttle & flux that had made the pine whole, & within
earshot of a muffled Macarena beat, beneath the plaid curtains

of the motel's second floor & branches ringed neon green,
I wonder what I'm doing here tonight. In Rome, I once saw
housed in locked vitrines rows of counterfeit relics, things

of this world that once meant *a correspondence* & now mean only
themselves. But that had seemed enough. How could it not —
each item chosen, swaddled in velvet, watched over

by the rented guards? As long as I stood there motionless & looked,
the thought even seemed sustainable. Fluorescent-lit clumps
of ribbon-knotted hair, wood splinters, & hand-forged nails. Each

cloth scrap & rosebush thorn, those touch-lustered livestock bones.

Line

Surface engraved with a narrow stroke, path

between two points. Of singular thickness, a glib remark,

fragment, an unfinished phrase. Any one edge of a shape

& its contours in entirety. Melody arranged, a recitation,

the way horizons are formed. Think of leveling, snaring,

the body's disposition (in both movement & repose).

It has to do with palms & creases, with rope wound tight

on a hand, things resembling drawn marks: a suture

or a mountain ridge, an incision, this width of light.

A razor blade at a mirror, tapping out a dose, or the churn

of conveyor belts, the scoured, idling machines. A conduit,

a boundary, an exacting course of thought. And here,

hammered-in tent stakes, shoveled earth, a trench.

Those Two Sketches by Severn in Italy

One, the one that no longer survives, is only of moonlight in Naples Bay —
widening, glistening in a chalk-colored sheet — & is, was, a stand-in
for the splendor of quarantine: ten days skittering with mast-stems & rigs,

the wings of sea birds & watching — stuffed with beef tongue, figs, & peaches —
hawkers, moorings, Vesuvius in haze, fishermen hauling in the inexhaustible
anchovy-like fish that from a distance was a silver writhing. Because

he had made already, ink-dipped stroke by stroke, at least a single thing
he saw pure — the look of black water suddenly aflame — there was no need,
perhaps, to render their vettura creeping towards Rome, how he heaped Keats

flat on his back with wildflowers — thistle, cyclamen & shrubby pimpernel,
those lavender petals neither one could name — or the heaps of water buffalo
grazing the hills, the lichen-covered rocks of aqueducts, roadside myrtle,

orange groves & gibbets, the sun-bleached severed arms of bandits. Because
moonlight was plenitude enough. And the other, that sketch of Keats's face —
adrift, sweat-slick, unshaved, done by oil lamp to stay awake — is enough, too,

of what Severn at last was made to admit: the rumpled locks plastered
to the forehead, that dark, unreadable, amorphous shape rising moon-like
from behind his cheek, & the sparse lines sprawling down from his neck

that mean, I know, *his breath in the dark,* but look like movement in water —
a current, a river, the churning sea, something like the storm that hatched
off Brighton when their cabin flooded from a leak in the planks & in the slosh

of gear squashing below Severn quipped *Here's pretty music for you* & the song
was only the *pails-full, waves,* he wrote, *in Mountains.* This sketch, too,
is those last months pared, distilled, & means *what seemed unending,* hours

of *fawn-colored* phlegm, the candlelit pages of *Holy Dying,* & afterwards,
that bonfire at the Spanish Steps after Signora Angeletti orders
the entire room burned — *beds, sheets, windows, doors,* even the bits

of wallpaper, varnish scraped from the floor, the ceiling's painted gold rosettes —
& how from all these gathered things the flames will lift, grow, & ash will fall
on the branches, the stone benches & stones, & settle in the fountain that is

Bernini's waterlogged boat sunk to its gunwale's fleshy curves, where water spills,
pours, perpetually from its sides with a sound that means *abundance, drowning.*

Part II

A Partial Invocation of Our Days

> Whereas God can make something from nothing, make
> something into nothing . . . human beings can only
> divide a thing into parts or assemble parts into a whole.
>
> — CAROLINE WALKER BYNUM

And yet, let's begin with macadam, fruit bowls, a Florentine mosaic,
Louie Louie's three slurred chords, & perhaps for now end there.

Since otherwise our days brim with dismantling, breakage, endless
riffs on the division into parts, I'll invoke here only assemblage:

buckets of sequins for a high school's *Tempest,* PBS splice
of the churning locust cloud. Next door, the sun-struck, mesa-culled

cow bones stacked near an adobe wall, & here this pile
of eraser shavings fingered into a line. Today let there be simply

plenitudes of making, a bravura of fabrications. O gathering
& uselessness. O panned seventies remake of *King Kong,*

with its six thousand pounds of Argentine horsehair stitched
to foam rubber & a hydraulic maze. I'm talking abundance

& the trivial, talking lies about the first *Kong,* too: if I omit
the metal facts of pulleys & cranes, a man on the set fastens

the furred paw to a pole & — deus ex machina — effortlessly works
the whole — arm over arm, smiling, all repose, easing a writhing

Fay Wray back through the shattered glass. Or anything held, clenched:
jury-rigged fort in a backyard elm; Edison, not this time plucking

newness from the void but, plagued by deafness & a love of the waltz,
gripping the Steinway's leg between his teeth to feel the melodies

resonate through his skull. Thus a trembling in three-quarter time.
The cinched & strand over strand. Barbwire, rubber bands, stamps.

What began as a brown tangle in a drawer becomes a massive ball
of twine. It was work. It was work that went on & on, consuming

the Midwest days. But look: now there's a plaque & a weight
upon the earth, *guaranteed twine to the core.* I'll take it — & still

whatever's clamped, held fast, sealed into a buttery worthlessness
like Sac City's two-ton popcorn globe, accrued, smashed, & pummeled

for hours into its roundish form. For this is the task. For this is what was
chosen to offer us joy: knitted V-neck cardigans; coyote fence posts

looped with wire; a pair of work boots snared in the telephone lines,
laced by a single knot into one dark, improbable shape.

Night Train: A Listener's Guide

Jimmy Forrest, sax man in the bandstand's back row,
tipped the tenor's bell, let his spit puddle out, & knew —
just months with Duke Ellington's band — he would pawn off

this riff as his own. He knew the sugared image
that inspired the song *Happy-Go-Lucky Local*
& thought *Fuck the fireman, the grin & nod, clang*

of a single bell. What he wanted was glassy-eyed,
raw, a growl — a spur line plowing Kansas City night,
battered, sputtering, a staccato wail, craving anything

within earshot. What he wanted would be Sonny Liston's
song of choice, shadowboxing, devouring the bag —
or, even closer, the champ years before, how he made

in St. Louis a rumbling of the night, jumping
packing-plant workers staggering home, arm-locked
couples interrupted midlaugh, the dockhand watching

the diner's sign flash between red & black. Between
Cole & Carr on Biddle Street, face broiled with ale,
Liston whips grit into the shop owner's eyes, swats him

down blinded with a single blow, kicks only twice
when the body stills, & finds nine ones in his sock. Listen
even closer: the man's telling the tale, crumpled, reeking

of sweat. He's trying again, stammering now, fumbling
to get everything right, & the cop's mind is on gas bills
& last night's game as he writes *overalls, 10:45,*

& pencils in next to Means of Attack: *Dirt, Fist, Feet.*

The Keeper of Hands

(the Kasai River, Congo Free State, 1898)

Updraft of air thickening,

        & what shifts

untouchable in wind,

        familiar, up from the river path,

stirred, from where

        the soldier grips

a fan of ostrich wing

        tied with a bit of lace. He

cools himself, sucks at

        his teeth, watches a barefoot

child tearing

        past, gazes at an insect

he cannot name

        flex its wings

on a rubber vine

        sticky with milky sap.

To count, assess, to stoke

        & prod, to keep

this moisture out. Above,

        the leaves that have

begun to wilt are yellowed

                    from the lift

of smoke. He must be sure

                    for each bullet used

there is a single right hand.

                    To smoke, to preserve.

He inspects the flames,

                    the framework of sticks,

the slats of heat & light.

                    With a knifetip he touches

a fist-sized shape.

                    They are all now

shriveled, blackened things.

                    They resemble

nothing he has ever seen.

Portrait of the Whirlwind in Job
as a Passenger Pigeon Flock

Roar of wings & the sky turned iridescent river

whirling through town upon town. There is wonder,

no doubt, & the silence due at what is beyond

knowing, at the marvelous thunder & our world

eclipsed by this veering inexhaustible mass

that is not an answer (for nothing had been asked)

but the air thick with a blaring multitudinous *I AM*.

Those who saw it — *serpent-shaped, a funnel-like*

leviathan cloud — will respond. With awe & a litany

of tools: tree-rigged mesh, hickory sticks, sulfur,

beer-drenched grain. Fire, shotguns, stones: our means

are nearly endless, too. It wheels on from here, thinning,

& countless rot in a freight car's heat & must be poured

into a ravine, & some are heaped on barges & hauled

downriver where they're sold fish-hooked on long cords.

The Scabbard of Limbs Means Flesh

In this version of the story, the work
is almost the same — at least in how
            it begins. The task of it, the means.

The shine of skin skinned back.
            Yet this one omits the muses,
the meager sweetness of the flute,

            & when what happens finally ends,
the river's dark water, thick with silt,
            remains wholly unchanged.

Someone has hand-colored the shot —
            its visible branches, the field behind,
the crowd's neckties, smirks. It's postmarked

            San Antonio, 1906, & in the photo
a girl clutches a darkened swatch of cloth
            she's torn loose as a souvenir. In the center,

in the foreground, two men
            have been kneeling for at least an hour
or now more than a hundred years.

            One tips his bowler, puffs a hand-carved pipe,
while the other mops sweat from his neck.
            With his mallet, his nails, & a kind

of nimble grace, he is careful not to split
            the barrel's staves, to methodically
space each one. The crowd waits — rapt, intent

— & does not look at the woman
at the postcard's edge, naked & strapped
        to a hackberry trunk by a belt & loop

of rope. No one, that is, except
        the cowlicked boy who grins & whispers
at her ear, who at any moment,

        one imagines, will exhaust things
to say & will only watch in silence
        as the nails pierce the cask & the uses

of the ordinary change.
        In order to describe the unspeakable
beauty of immaculate light,

        Dante calls upon Apollo: *Come
into my breast & breathe there,
        as when thou drewest Marsyas*

from the scabbard of his limbs.
        Which is to say Marsyas was skinned alive,
his body turned into a single wound.

        Apollo leaned in, attuned to his work
for hours, even after he was asked,
        Why do you tear me from myself?

Because this is what he chose to do.
        Which is to say in San Antonio
this is how they began, too. They began

        at her feet with a pocketknife
but either grew bored or perhaps
        understood they weren't quite the same

as the gods. Yet there was time.

        There is time & they turn to other things,
& since we have only ourselves,

        our flesh, our metaphors for skin,
the myth is nearly useless by now.
        What happened was this: they finished

tapping in the nails & sealed the barrel shut
        with the woman inside, who remained,
for a while, alive. And several times

        in what must have been laborious work
a group of them watched or helped roll it back
        up from the river to the hill.

        Forget the gods & the body as one wound.

An East Toledo Map of Ash

What about simply these sun-warmed stones, backlit leaves, two jays

gobbling apricots within reach? But you're picturing an oil drum brimming
    with flames, the way trash braids into smoke: pastel plastic hangers,

cans, a punctured hose, a framed sketch of orchids streaming from black grass,

    black bags cinched with twine, & how ash drifts off to the gutters & oaks,
the curbstones, fences & vines. How even if the wind were suddenly to shift,

    or these ash-flakes became more sustainable things, you couldn't watch them

hover for a bit, fluttering, adrift, or float now two blocks away, where
    they might settle on the shoulders of a pimpled boy who today believes,

after making the Creeper, One-Handed Velvet Rolls, a flawless Slippery Eel,

    that he can become, with a single Twist the Atom Behind the Back,
Toledo's East Side Yo-yo Champ. And here you are now, doing this again,

    guessing at lives & aftermath, tracing ash to take you where? Somewhere —

does it matter? — you might have paused once or stayed, perhaps a room down
    at the Motel 6 from where a girl, high on polish & glue, allows the remains

of her ashtray to sail in slow arcs to the floor. Out on the sidewalk,

    some kids are skipping rope, chanting little rhymes about steamboats & fudge,
silver buttons, a piece of glass. *Bridges, ashes, falling down.* A man half tanked

at a traveling fair scrawls his name in the salt he spilled, then pays to see a mermaid,

glistening with scales & Vaseline, smoke & tail-twitch in a tub. Someone
touches a blade of grass to a fire pit, someone chooses the leaf-green urn. Tonight,

the guard at North Star Steel will watch the Mudhens lose, 15–3, then drive

with his daughter over the Maumee to the docks, sure the time is now. The air is filled
with what only he can see & he knows the world begins to burn. Until

they both slip into darkness, far from anyone's sight, you'll pretend to see them

paddle ineptly from the shore, the girl bailing lake water in little S-shaped curves
& the man, for some reason, stopping again, trying match after wind-blown match.

In a moment you won't even try to hear his tuneless, half-remembered lullabies,

the irregular splash of his oars, or the sound of all the provisions he packed —
bits of tuna fish & ash-gray dough — dribbling over the boat's side, where some

break apart in moonlight or — unwatched, unseeable — float for a while in the waves.

Thumb Trick

Houdini, bored in a New York cab, stalled midtown with the Doyles,
displays his hand perfectly intact, makes a plucking sound with his tongue,

      & removes the first joint of his thumb.

In that pause before everything is again made whole, Lady Doyle sags
limp against the glass, & Sir Arthur, stunned, fumbles for words, broods

      on *our miraculous acts.* Once

locked in Memorial Day traffic, my father showed us the same trick.
Watch this, he said, *I think something's changed,* & in mock awe

      at what the body can do, severed,

then reattached his flesh. We all wanted the secret immediately, to unfasten
ourselves the same way. For Doyle, it only proves what he knew:

      the ease with which the body can be

joined by the air between. Each night in his Diary of Manifestations,
he lists the impossible he's seen: piles of jellyfish & Moroccan coins,

      panther skin, turf & jewels,

& once, webbed in seaweed, a hammerhead thrashing the séance table.
He explains how heaven resembles our world — *lawns, paved walks,*

      geometry, tangerines — & how each

of our earthly selves is paired with an ethereal form. That summer
at the Lake Erie tourist traps, a billboard lured me in — *Bottomless!*

The Unfathomable Deep! —

& I dropped my two-dollar allowance on admission to the Blue Hole.
I clutched my torn ticket stub & made my way to the rail, desirous,

of course, uneasy, sure

everything was about to change. Maybe we're only what we offer ourselves to,
what we choose to want to believe. Like Doyle transcribing each time

his son has risen from the dead —

once to part his father's lips; once, trembling, to touch his wrist. To the rapt
crowd at Carnegie Hall, he shows photos of the spirits' realm. A hallway

with something indiscernible midair,

a hovering diaphanous face, winged Yorkshire fairies weaving a nest,
& one he knew *beyond all fraud:* a church scene in London on Armistice Day

snapped in the two-minute prayer —

the pews, the minister, the organ, stained glass, &, airborne, awash with light,
a dozen bodiless heads. *These are,* he makes clear, *our dead returned, a rippling*

from the other world.

And from the Blue Hole's edge? The smell of chlorine, a ribboned glare, deepening
gradations of blue. *It's unending,* I made myself think. Even after they recognize

all of Doyle's war dead,

he still manages to believe. A few were jockeys in London's East End, alive,
still working the tracks. Another, clipped from a local sports page: a man looking

baffled, enraged — taken

from the time he sliced the ball & scored into his own team's net. And one
of the dead was Battling Siki, who lives on to rise with his windmill punch

& become Champion of the World.

Who lives on to lose the Belt to McTigue, to be kayoed, to give up the ring,
to stagger Harlem aimless, loose with gin, with a fez-capped lion on a leash.

Doyle writes in his diary, *The unimaginable*

surrounds us each day, & Siki finds it in pool halls, tumblers of bootleg rye,
his whippet backflipping on cue. And a few months before Houdini is killed

by a man's sucker punch to the gut,

Siki, ablaze in headlights, hearing someone slurring his name, will be shot
in the back for a twenty-dollar debt, will be buried in Flushing, Queens.

Licking the El Greco

Out of tribute, sheer badness, adolescent gall, or just because the guard then turned:
entirely across a hill's moss-green curve, a friend leans in & licks the El Greco

& thus *The Agony in the Garden* glistens through an otherwise aimless afternoon.
This is something he's wanted for years, & how often is desire perfectly fulfilled,

especially in Toledo, Ohio, especially in this painting's particular world
where a man, put upon by a fawning angel, kneels in the brush-stroked grass

while, in the distance — only a few inches away — the clump of soldiers begin,
as they always will, slow, purposeful steps? How else to inhabit that

undulating stone, the blanket's steel-blue bustled furl, white streaks standing in
for celestial light bleaching crimson robes to plum? To offer up mildly to no one

again, *Hmmmm,* meaning *there's pleasure in those blurred, steamy billows of sky,
this cramped & nebulous space, those stylized ash-gray hands?* No: far better

to find ways of approximating saying, to lunge, for instance, the tongue's wet tip,
to manage, lamely, a flick of consecration, to respond to human touch with touch.

A Blues About Wanting in the End

In a Chicago warehouse, in a cinderblock room, a voice
calls & doesn't latch to words & thus is *longing*

perfectly said. Rapturous, honeyed
with wanting, weaving towards a chorused groan,

a single hum grows — beckoning, aflame —
& two beats behind the drummer's pulse of sixteenths,

two others, frenzied, begin. On the next take
they'll add lyrics again — *I roll & tumble, baby, cry*

the whole night long. When I woke up this morning, baby,
all I had was gone — but for now the melody

is only three grinning, insatiable wails, having not much
to do with harmony except desires that are pitched the same.

～

There's Luke Killeck at twelve, down at the tracks,
teaching us how, with his waterlogged porn,

to peel each page delicately back & keep the glossy bodies
intact. How to hold our smokes we filched from the store

& how, when we sloshed gasoline on the Fosslers' lawn,
sun scorched what it touched to straw.

Like pissing words, he said, *in snow.* All day,
we scoped their yard from the crabapple, waiting

～

for our names to burn in, to show themselves at last. Or
there's my neighbor this morning, sipping at a Pabst,

counting the piñon dying in his yard, each tree's skeletal remains.
He tells me again, *They're coming. They're everywhere*

& there's nothing we can do. He's tried: slow-drip tubing,
pesticide jugs, trunks hacked down & mulched

as soon as the branch tips turn, slash heaps hauled off
the same day. He tries counting this time the stumps

left behind but trails off before he's done & in the silence
I say nothing of the beginnings of beauty, the look

of this engraver beetle's work. Through the long distance
of today's afternoon, a chainsaw's steady grind. Pickups

topheavy with roped heaps of wood trundle down our road.
By now I've swiped a branch from a dun-colored stack

& gently begun with a pocketknife
to pry its bark back. Because I wanted to see:

the wood honeycombed, scar-sprawled & furrowed;
the tangle of channels where the larvae have hatched,

slivered rivulets where they've fed. Sometimes
by *engraved* we mean *devoured.* Once,

~

sandwiched in the porn in Luke's lockbox,
we found a damp, titleless book thick with recipes

for homemade bombs. In an instant the ordinary changed —
what was possible, within grasp. That night,

we swaddled mothballs into newspaper scraps,
lit one by one our homemade wicks, & pitched

what the book called *Makeshift Napalm* at traffic
on Cotter's Road, forming from the cattails piles of flames

that smoldered, widened, & at last adhered as a green-edged blaze
to a station wagon's swerving wheels. In one telling

⁓

of the story, when the war's slaughter for an evening stops,
Helen reaches out with a slim freckled hand & touches

the horse's wooden belly, hearing, perhaps,
from somewhere within, the clank of bodies shifting inside,

gold plates rubbing engraved gold. Or parts of flesh
or timber, spears passed from hand to hand.

She moves barefoot between the horse's legs & all
the stars that are shaped like a man carrying a sword

have dipped well below the sea. Other than these men
packed into wood, in the courtyard she's alone. Her fingers

pass across each carved fir rib as she purrs & whispers their names.

What I Mean When I Say Blossom

is, yes, stargazers clumped in a vase & this morning beginning
to unfold, or the mesa's cobalt irises trying to engulf the withered
field. But also a boy slumped at a wall, lifting the gas-soaked rag

to his face, a burn mark — I can't help it — curving across a thigh
& that air raid photograph, taken moments after, in which the land, too,
seems to bloom. There's a drawing Scotch-taped to my freezer,

scribbled in mulberry & teal, of Saint Dorothy clasping daisies
petaled with lowercase *u*'s, or there's the Wal-Mart security screen
I watched become awash with backdrop light, effloresce, & turn

entirely white each time the doors hissed back & someone — looking
for a blender or butterscotch-scented candles — stepped into
the kind of bright, tiled space by now we can't live without. Within

Rorschach ink blot VIII alone, patients have seen coral reefs, baskets,
a bladder, a woman weeping who wears a green hat, Jell-O, Greenland,
fir tree in the distance, a coat of arms, iridescence of a bubble. Odd,

how I'm reluctant to give up this list, how it's easier to tell you
salamander, labia, ribs laid open, forest fire & canoe, even
Mother Goose without a neck, than finish what I'm trying to say.

Let's allow tonight, for as long as we can, for this word instead
to empty itself until it is nothing but sweetness & petals, until it means
only twilight, pear-white sand, our tongues thick with palm liquor.

Or only the mail-order orchid we keep not far from our bed. Each evening
at dusk — although it's futile & we're miles from any such thing —
it tries to lure a nocturnal moth by filling our room with its scent: citrus,

or cinnamon, or jasmine — we haven't quite placed it yet. No matter.
Our bodies will soon begin to move, or perhaps lie perfectly still,
& for a while I won't need the name of anything at all to be clearer.

Part III

Shapes of Stone & Prayer

Once, you pressed a palm-sized stone into my hand,
asked me to pray on it for you, & left me with a silence

I could feel seizing the room. You wanted only
faith to compress & a single thing to grip, but I couldn't even

count the things I wished I could believe. Afterwards,
unsure of what shapes my hands should make, I could only

raise feebly, facing the moon-washed lawns, a glass to the night,
to the handful of stars that remained. At your memorial,

again & again, they raised the Bible into air,
& the minister's words, untroubled, exact, described all

of what you could see: pearl, sapphire, a sea of glass,
white linen, pages of names. I am tired of being told

what the dead wear, what verbs encompass their acts:
they awaken, they choose & clasp. My friend, you are gone

from here & missed & the silence now has changed.
What I hold tonight, instead of those words, is yet another stone

to touch with no end in mind. What I'm guessing at
you must already know: that its one black & mottled edge

might be a form blessing could take & that to trace
its one trembling, fissured line entirely around could be

an act of intercession, or some kind of prayer in itself.
To finger all of this stone's syllables its unvarying weight may have.

for JT

Trenton, a Solmization, Two Rivers, a Few Tells

The woman seated behind me on the train hums the same notes again
& again. There are only two pitches in the pattern she's latched to

& for some reason can't let go. It's been the same through six towns now —
just two notes emphatic & hushed with only a small flux between them

as if a pattern of ascension, pause, & return were melody enough.
I glance back & see her eyes are shut, that her hands move in rhythm, too.

They open, palms up, hesitate, & clench. Pause, then open again. A voice
from the speakers announces the next stop & once more clips short the name.

Now arriving in Lin — is all any of us hear before static stifles it out.

                                         Today, in Trenton,
in a poker game, I will sit & lose piles of plastic chips, & as I listen

to this woman repeat once again notes that are barely a song, I wish
there was something else to tell you, that this moment might somehow

clasp a weight that wields more than this frivolous game.

                                                   I could be moving
south on this train because of a note I pulled damp from the trash, a room

at the Starlite Motel, or perhaps some implacable loneliness I can't explain
or even understand. Because it's not enough, is it, to hear a woman hum,

that some of the names I pass through are trimmed to *Rah* & *Tol,* that I'll lose
hands of anaconda, guts?

                    In Düsseldorf, in a winter storm, in 1849, Emanuel Leutze

began to paint George Washington crossing the river into Trenton. To ready himself
he studied the Rhine through whole afternoons, sketching for hours surface & crest,

its illegible flow & surge. The slabs of ice he carted in & arranged on mats of straw
softened slowly by the oil lamps as he practiced catching a glistening that was beautiful

& meant nothing. *By the time it was finished, it nearly killed me,*
Washington's stand-in moaned, & at the end, no longer able to grip his spyglass,

he collapsed drunk into the makeshift boat.
                                            Once, I even saw it — the crossing —
reenacted in a Sea World tank our bicentennial year: the whale trainer grinning

in his gray wetsuit, his black tricorn hat, one arm waving a plastic flag
as he balanced on the back of Shamu.
                            Someone who beats me at poker claims

we all have consistent tells. An ice cube clink, jawbone clench, a finger tap,
a sigh. He means, I suppose, the body's compulsions will always give voice

to our lies.
            In Leutze's painting, it's morning, the day after Christmas,
1776. Washington, taut, regal in his whaler, is fixed on the opposite shore.

Leutze, of course, knew the real crossing took place in a battered shallow-draft scow
& that, given where his sun rises in the dawn, the men are lit with an impossible light.

He had his methods, reasons.
                                    Would it matter if I told you there was no card game,
that I made most of this up? That even if it's true the woman sang a few notes,

that was months ago, & it's only now, I swear, they seem like a reply to a question
I've never managed to ask? Concise. Irrefutable.
                                    In the eleventh century,

Guido of Arezzo broke each phrase from a hymn to Saint John & assigned
each syllable a note. *Ut,* he began, then inscribed *re,* each pitch progressing

from the one before. The rising, the exactness, the *mi* & *fa* & *sol* — all arranged
for what he called a passing through, as one moves through the days of the week.

Which is to say, yes, it is Sunday again, a day resembling any Sunday before
only in resonance & name. And if it's true the monk later chose the human hand

to map out a place for each pitch, then perhaps I don't need to say anything more
of rivers, or ice, or whales. Of lies, of names ending too soon. Even of those notes

repeated & hummed that never reached towards a melody, but lingered as a moment
within one, absolved from constraints of song. Then perhaps I could stop

& point to this knuckle, this fingertip here, & you'd know exactly what I mean.

Patio Lull with House Guest & View

If Leonardo could find in his mildew-splotched walls
not only the horizons of haze-smudged hills, valley-sprawl
dark with spring bloom, but fields
                                of crosshatched, sword-wielding men
milling about where a scribble of catapults begins, perhaps I can find

a path through today's now-ebbing drone of lost euchre tricks,
talk of work, this drought, more drinks, & manage to seize upon
not some grandiose turn
                                from jaundiced house-rot to the pastoral ablaze,
but a bit of the actual, some proffered-up what-have-you. It's not easy:

wren-colored dirt, patio stones, margarita salt freckling my father's lip
&, beyond where he now dozes at last, the luminous orange flare
of a surveyor's ribbon tight on a hammered stake. Even then, I know:
what of it? What can this meager seeing amount to, watching

the day's last ravens belly-skim the pines, one twilight star beelining west
that I'll follow for as long as I can bear before turning back once again
to that Chevy crawling past, its driver bellowing, *Buster, Buster,*
both syllables slackened to a plaintive cry that resembles nothing

in the language? In Leonardo's earliest drawing — *On the Feast
of Saint Mary of the Snow, 1473* — the visible engulfs the whole page.
This is the first landscape for its own sake, & rather than banishing
our clamored-after world
                                to backdrop for flesh nailed to wood,

here it is returned — shrubs, fissured oxbowed rocks, waterfall
loosened to mist. Yet this, too, is less about precision than a view
billowed with what dazzles the mind. Thus curlicue scrub
tumbles into smoke, trees paddlewheel air, & an April stillness

froths & swirls like batter as if
                                        squirming from his gaze. But how
to render this dimly lit stuff before me — brick, gravel, bird I can't name,
grill cover rippling in wind — or make it serve some inscrutable need
which anything retrieved must do? What might be salvaged anyway,

within one pause & a half-assed stare, before the mind skids off
from the evergreen at hand & returns to my father, snug
in his lounge chair straps, artichoke dip on his shirt, wanting
nothing more as night & kitchen-clatter grow, & seeing

nothing, too, until, I imagine,
                              his mind flits back just now
to the one winter as a boy he'd thread the same twelve blocks,
past Pawn City, Lucky's Liquors, Glazed Hams & More, to reach
Red Goose Shoes' fluoroscopic gimmick: an x-ray device

on the store's main floor in which he would place both feet,
flip a rubber switch, & pretending to check for the sneaker's fit,
access a window *through*. How easy then
                                        to see it, after a steadiness,
a whir: flesh gleaming in a pulpit-shaped box, the seen now

changed in that green glow into something boundless, incandescent.

Swallowed Things

(after the collection of Dr. Chevalier Jackson)

Fish bones & seeds. A toothpick, pipe stems. Two legibly inscribed jade rings.

The body must be

recumbent, facing downward, with lowered shoulders & head. A thimble, coal lump,

a pistachio shell,

peach pits, a tin whistle half. *Do not, lest it be further pushed into the larynx,*

try to reach for it

with your hand. A penny, a jack, kernels of some kind. A key that must have been

fingered, considered,

passed across a pair of lips. Emblems of accident — bullet casings, bottle caps,

that winking doll head —

or erratic compulsion — pottery shards, the spoon. *Carefully consider the texture,*

each object's size & shape.

Consider Mary N ——, age 23, who could finally return to the stocking factory

once the lead button

was removed. Or Brooks G ——, who had lodged for seven years an Audubon badge

in his bronchus.

Monitor weight loss, the fever's range. A hinge, a tack while laying down

oilcloth, the jeweled

locket of Dorothy K ——, somehow the clock's cogged wheels. As if

almost a way

of transforming the ordinary, making sacrament of what's within reach.

This movement

from, say, a safety pin, to this one, here, this particular thing, you now

survived & hold.

To a Student Who Refuses to Read More
of *The Inferno* After Learning None of It Is True

Pliny tells us Zeuxis rendered the grapes with such care
crows circled back all afternoon to peck at the work he'd done.

This though, too, is just a story of seeming &, like the other, untrue.
I need to tell you about the sweetness of the lie, or how

Pliny once likened a foxtail to a dangling cluster of grapes —
does it matter if the metaphor is botched? Only last century scientists believed

masses of migrating insects caused the dark spots on the moon. Although
they, too, never went there, imagine for a moment the swarm & hum,

shadows alive with writhing, those gathered & countless wings. The lie
is exactly the point in Caravaggio's *Basket of Fruit.* There are the windfallen,

worm-rot, slit fig skins, grapes dust-caked & flecked with white —
these things are, & they are other. What I mean is not the world

returned, but how artifice corresponds to the exact: the way this light
& lack of shadow don't quite add up, these arbitrary leaf silhouettes,

or how the table on which the basket rests seems to relinquish
its attempt to seem & dissolves into a stroke of brown paint.

When Howard Thurston, performing the Temple of Love, allows
a woman to roam the air, only one boy will be plucked from the audience

to join the magician on stage. To ensure beyond doubt the miraculous,
to prove Princess Fernanda rises without any support. And when her body

ascends & *vanishes like a cloud,* we know now Thurston will lift
the boy towards the lights & whisper solemnly in his ear,

If you touch any of those fucking wires, I'll toss you from this goddamn stage —
evoking, as needed, speechlessness, wide eyes, a slackened mouth.

Do I need to say *allegory, terza rima, stars*? Or how, in the canto
where the eighth bolgia begins, without the likening of bodies

wholly consumed to the moment when a man gathering grapes
pauses to watch the fireflies rise in a midsummer night

we'll know nothing of the wounded flesh? Perhaps even nothing
of the indisputable: the ooze & actual softening, the pulp & grape itself.

A Damaged Fresco of *The Massacre of the Innocents*

There must be something to be said for the pattern ruin makes,
or for anything that seems like a remnant of touch,

a stark coalescence of light. In this fresco, at its bottom edge,
the dead are layered & stacked where they were tossed,

rendered in a heap of limbs: body piled on body, flesh
crowding other flesh — all of it blunt & simply told just as it is

in Neruda's poem, when his description of geraniums
& sunlight ends & then *The blood of children flowed*

easily in the street like the blood of children, denying
the ornaments of language, the idea that for everything

something must correspond. Yet in this fresco everything
seems & *resembles,* & the bodies of these children can't help

but correspond to the various things of this world. Look:
each strand of ambered hair is like the feathered tips of crow wings

catching the light, & their flesh is like the color of rising bread,
weathered piles of stone, or even a landscape's receding curves,

its hills tumbling into the horizon. Perhaps it's only
the sky's ultramarine that suggests solely itself, blue

in a contiguous, purified form . . . and yet, in the fresco's center,
the blue is worn & falling away in an elegant, vein-like collapse

& because a bare white patch of plaster beneath circles the shape
of a child's outstretched hand — each knuckle & finger, the thumb's

delicate web — it reminds me of those monastery paintings I've seen
in which the eyes of the saints have all been scratched out:

the color used is believed to restore sight to the blind.
And what about this fresco's sky? Was the pigment that surrounds

this painted flesh trimmed away, too, out of the same impulse of faith,
a precise & human touch? Doubtful. More likely, this spot of fragile wear

has more to do with plaster improperly slaked or the ease
with which acids corrode aquamarine. Alkalines, the damp,

efflorescence & salt, the inevitable loosening of tone. All of this
I know. But bear with me. I want to forget what is *likely* for now,

I want to linger in only what *seems:* the pattern here, this flawlessness,
the places of meticulous transparency, its hued & refining sheen.

Because all of the other colors here — burnt umbers, ochres,
viridians, & reds — & the objects they depict are still impeccably intact:

mullioned windows, the foreground of earth, each blade & cloak.
As if we did need only to touch — deftly, repeatedly —

where pigment renders sky, each place it borders with flesh.

Audubon Diptych

I. Wherein the Swallows Instruct Us in Pleasure

Because they daubed with poppy sap the stricken eyes of their young
& because each thin body, it was believed, contained a bright red stone
that could honey the word-addled tongue, balm the frenzied brain,

they were restorers, the ancients taught.
                                        And were the restored, too,
since year after year farmers observed them, just after the autumn frost,
plummet single-file, like a bead of pearls, into lakes where they remained

submerged until spring when they'd wing back in dripping columns.
All of which is no less improbable than Audubon's account
of the slate-green birds pouring into a sycamore trunk *like bees*

hurrying into their hive. The thunder of wings in this slow inhalation —
for the tree seemed to breathe in bird upon bird — was first matched
by thunder building behind the Silver Hills, & then was paired, once

he pressed his ear to the bark, with the delicate clamor & scratch
of each one inching through the hollow. *Those wings,*
                                        he imagined,
by my lantern's light, & until his light possessed them, what use

to see them merely thread the air? What use were the half-done sketches
of his flycatcher, grouse, that for-now-unworkable clapper rail beak
& hearing, instead of their ravishing wing-frenzied stream, jam jars rattling

on the boil? Thus a hired woodsman pries back the bark & allows him
one night to burrow in.
                        Who wouldn't want this too? To stand within
the tree's eight-foot trunk & gaze upon them teeming in rows?

To reach into, as he did, the crushed-quill mat & pluck them from sleep
& kill — soundlessly, with a kind of care — as many as he could carry?
Closing the entrance, Audubon concludes, *we marched towards Louisville,*

perfectly elated.

 And despite where his story is hard to believe, no one doubts
this joy. For what could have been lacking, that journey home? There was
the road's moonlit, moss-webbed oak, seen as if for the first time

& here in his pockets, filled to bursting, the slender, still-warm forms.

II. Resurrection & the Common Merganser

Before he could restore even one part — tail-plunge, talon tips
sunk into catfish flesh & whatever it is that makes his warbler
weightless on the azalea stem — Audubon invariably failed. To make,

as was always his plan, the watercolors' stippled touch return
the quick breaths
 of each bird. He tried first with a pigeon slung
against a barn door, but even if he managed its burnt-orange throat,

he could only render it as it was before him: gangly in a one-legged splay.
And before he pummeled it to pieces — humbled, irate — he tried
to build a Universal Bird, a manikin of cork & narrow wooden stumps

barely reminiscent of wings, let alone a kind of flight. But life,
he believed, could be brushstroked back & he blundered towards
nimbler forms.
 Aesacus, hidden within another story, can no longer watch

river water pearl on Hesperia's skin, & so pursues her, lust-driven,
through the fields & woods until death reaches for her ankle
in the slender form of a snake. Only then do his desires change

& when he flings himself, guilt-stricken, headlong from the cliff,
a god, as the gods will rarely do, denies him the privilege of death.
This time, Ovid tell us, the body doesn't change in a whirlwind fit

but rather, as Aesacus plunges down towards the waves, feathers
pierce his skin. Before long he'll become the first merganser,
the same crested fish-diving duck
                              Audubon clips almost daily

from the Mississippi's iced-over banks. Of one he notes
its triangular tongue, the nine-inch bottom-feeder lodged in its gut,
that its legs were, as usual, the color of sealing wax, & then begins

to rekindle its life through the method by then he'd learned: first, impale
with wire the sun-dried wings, its mandible & mottled breast; attach it
to a plank with a backdrop grid & mold it to a lifelike pose. Odd,

how in the watercolors for *The Birds of America,* we're missing
the engraver's final work: the river is just a few light-blue strokes
& instead of an intricate tangle of grass, a merganser soars

through an empty page. Aesacus,
                              for a while, isn't finished either,
though he will be soon. Even as he thrashes in his rage & grief,
not quite bird or man, he can feel it, the lure of it beginning

in his beginning-to-be-hollow bones. What else can he do
but unburden himself, give himself over to the body's suppleness,
its impossible glistening, the grace afforded after all?

Towards the Sound of a Heron Stepping on Ice

February mist, morning thaw just begun, & the heron that is the same
color of slate as the pond on which she moves

                                        today is nowhere in sight.
Two days ago, my wife & I watched her hunting near the drainage pipe

& heard at first nothing at each supple step. Then, just as her foot touched,
a muffled creak of something

                        giving way, her body's weight pressing
at ice. We lost track of how long this lasted: patternless, a few steps

of audible silence, surface

                        giving nothing back, & then — cleanly,
sporadically — a tap of pressure on the ice's crust. She was stalking
God knows what, moving on a pond frozen through — slow, determined,

then lingering, affixed

                        on something we couldn't see. A heron hunting
tucks one leg back, lifts its neck, & with a sudden stab through air,
allows its body to unfold. This one, though, I've only seen take

these tentative steps, lean in, wait implausibly, then begin
moving again. What happened

                        ～

                        took place weeks after
Isadora Duncan's children drowned & isn't much of a story at all.

This was after the driver turned the stalled car's crank & the vehicle
lurched & tumbled down the embankment, broke the river's surface,
& was gone. Somewhere

                        on a beach on Corfu, Duncan imagines

the Seine's ribboned gray — its surge

                                      & gradual calm — & pictures

hooks & dragging lines, an anchor snagged on a sun-glazed wheel.

Then, although she's promised *there will be nothing more,*

she watches her arm move. Wave froth, sand fleas, beach grass scruff.

Her hand lowered, raised. It seems, perhaps, like the first gesture

she has made

                      as she bends her wrist gradually back & makes what the body does

willed: for a moment, almost, mending, evanescence, her body

both forgotten & salve to itself, & then fastened to a way of saying

that somehow seems to suffice. For years,

                                     ~

                             a man born in a stubble field

is satisfied documenting his walks. *It is,* he claims, *our flawless art,*

just as it's perfect

                how dust freckles each lemon tree blossom, or how

his horses stir in their decrepit stalls, watching rain pool in the dark palm

of a shovel & in the earth

                    between their hooves. These are moments

the man considers, too, as he drifts through the streets & hills, taking

endless pictures of himself doing ordinary things, stark naked in each one.

Catching his breath at a barbwire fence, waiting for a passing mule.

Striding past a silo, scattering ravens. Arms outstretched, leaping from a rock.

Sipping walnut brandy in the shade.

                          A friend once tried to explain this to me,

defining it in terms of dailiness, ritual, the precarious
framework of the mundane. *Think of Duchamp's urinal,* I was told.
Or Rauschenberg's *Erased de Kooning,*

                                    a piece in which absence, fixed

in a gold-leaf frame, becomes
                            an end in itself. In which absence takes
the form of a yellow sheet clumped with remnants of ink & crayon. It's not
the same, is it, as that story of Pollock, most likely far from true?

How he once bought a Picasso in order to erase it, to learn
how the line might work,
                        the way the body's dialect finds voice.
Lead on cream paper, c. 1908. *Four Studies of the Human Hand.*

Then his task filled hours — each fingertip, knuckle,

                            ∽

                                    wrist. In a photo
taken somewhere in Russia, a crowd lunges towards a train window,
eager for the papers offered by a boy, hardly caring they're mostly lies.

But now here is the reason we look at it, why it was preserved:
in the window next to this boy someone has been painted out.
Airbrushing, cropping, faces
                        ink-smudged or excised with a razor —

it was all common, we know. Except here the work is so poorly done
it looks deliberate — how the black of the window barely blends
with the space where his body should be
                                    & all of his contours

are clear. At his torso, the oval construct of his head, each brushstroke
is so thick & obvious, patterned
                                                        in thumbprint whorls, it resembles
proportion lines from some *How to Draw* book. Symmetries, ratios,

augmented angles, methods to ensure
                                                    each of the parts is in harmony
with the whole. It's as if whoever removed him from this scene
was only beginning to understand just how the body works —

its axis, his shoulder's traversing lines, that single mark
from scalp to ribs.
                        Polyclitus knew *the beautiful comes about*
little by little, through many numbers, & perhaps with our rules

for rendering ourselves
                                    mimesis is nothing but math. Perhaps, too,
this work was botched in order that we might notice, might begin
to guess. That this man who stared down half asleep from the train

was the same man who once seared his brother's eyes with a rust-flecked awl
then walked from his home without a word. Who, one night, was made to kneel
in the woods when his throat was slit

                                    ∼

                                    beneath the pines. Done in one take,

forty seconds long, the first film ever made — *Lunch Hour at the Lumière Factory* —
shows only a crowd
                            walking into sunlight, hurrying into a blazing lane.
There's a rush of wool dresses, hand placed into a pocket, a shrug,

a mastiff's fevered joy. Behind & above, back in the rafters: the pure
geometry of light & wood.
                              At the climax, a girl plucks at her button
& a black horse trots nimbly by, harnessed to a cart covered in canvas

that gives back as it passes
                              the shadowed branches of an oak. By now
it's December, 1895. In a Paris basement salon, a crowd watches
the image of a crowd projected on a pinned white sheet. A machine whirs

& rattles along with the same effort of its name — *cinématographe,*
from the Greek, meaning *writing the movement.* They watch
soundless blacksmiths striking at steel,
                              the lift & curve of waves,

& then a passenger train that glides into a station & seems to them,
at least in one story, like artifice

                              ⌒

                              for a single breath more. Muybridge,
I've read, invented moving pictures by making a horse circle a track.

First it galloped & broke each thread laced across its path,
which in turn tripped the camera shutters & told us how it moved —
how its body curved, lagged, compressed,
                              & how there were moments,

indiscernible, when not a hoof touched the earth.
                              A few years after
he hunted down his wife's lover playing cribbage at a Calistoga mine
& shot him point-blank in the chest, Muybridge made

naked dancers & gymnasts move against a grid of white lines.
Here is *A Man Walking*
                              and Turning. A Man Heaving a Boulder.
Carrying a Rifle. Digging with a Spade. A Woman Drying Her Feet. Listen:

there's no better time to finish one story I began before. It's about the artist
who roamed the village hills & I'm not even sure it's true: when war came,
the man arranged to end his walks
                              & put his camera away. Instead, he began

to choose. He chose which of the dead he would allow to be buried,
which rottweiler, woman, which ear. To make
                              some move barefoot
towards an idling truck, then bedsprings, truncheons, stones. But listen:

in one series of Muybridge photographs, a woman approaches a chair.
She is naked, in profile, & beginning to move
                              closer to its curved pine back.
She is the same woman who pours a single glass of water, who stands

after sitting on the floor. This time, though, she takes a few steps, kneels
at a chair, pauses,
                    then rises again. She has either a look of solemnity
or a half-smile latched to her face — because she knows

what she is about to do.
                              By the fifth frame we can see it, almost
in entirety, & she touches it with her knuckle. This is *A Woman Kneeling
at a Chair,* & somewhere within or near the eighth frame —

since this is all she intends — gesture & desire
                              coalesce. She lowers
her body, clasps her hands, in one motion bowing her head,
& even if this lasts for just a fractured second she seems

to be honestly in prayer. As if not kneeling *at* but *to* a chair. Adamant,
resolved. As if there were nothing else to kneel to. As if knowing
in a moment she will be finished & begin to rise

but for now it is still not yet.

"Small Blessing for a Child," it turns out, is for Cyrus.

"Montezuma's Painters": I first learned of Montezuma's platoon of artists from David D. Perlmutter's *Visions of War*.

"Line" is for Phillis Levin.

"Those Two Sketches by Severn in Italy" is based on several accounts of Keats's journey to Rome, especially his letters, the letters of Joseph Severn, and Aileen Ward's *John Keats: The Making of a Poet*.

"*Night Train:* A Listener's Guide": for some of the facts contained here, I am indebted to *The Devil and Sonny Liston* by Nick Tosches. The poem is for William Appling.

"The Keeper of Hands" owes a debt to *King Leopold's Ghost*, Adam Hochschild's haunting history of Belgian forces in the Congo.

"The Scabbard of Limbs Means Flesh": the lines quoted from Dante are taken from John D. Sinclair's translation of *Paradiso*. The lynching in this poem is based on an incident mentioned in Philip Dray's *At the Hands of Persons Unknown*.

"Thumb Trick" is for Kathy Graber. Some of the details about Arthur Conan Doyle's spiritualism are based on events recounted in Kenneth Silverman's biography of Houdini.

"A Blues About Wanting in the End": the opening section refers to a 1950 recording of "Rollin' and Tumblin'" by Little Walter, Baby Face Leroy, and Muddy Waters.

"What I Mean When I Say Blossom" includes some of the patients' readings of ink blots as noted in Samuel J. Beck's *Rorschach's Test*.

"Shapes of Stone & Prayer" is for Jen Turek.

"To a Student Who Refuses to Read More of *The Inferno* After Learning None of It Is True": Jim Steinmeyer reveals the truth about Thurston's levitation trick in his book *Hiding the Elephant*.

"Swallowed Things": this poem takes a few liberties with Dr. Chevalier Jackson's actual collection of swallowed things as well as his texts on surgery of the throat. This group of objects, arranged in drawers in Philadelphia's Mütter Museum, comprises more than two thousand items the surgeon removed from patients' throats.

"A Damaged Fresco of *The Massacre of the Innocents*": Giotto's fresco depicting this scene is in the Arena Chapel in Padua, Italy. The lines from Pablo Neruda are taken from his poem "I Explain a Few Things."

"Audubon Diptych": Some of the italicized phrases were taken from Audubon's encounter with these swallows as described in his *Ornithological Biography*. I am also grateful to Richard Rhodes's biography of the artist and Audubon's *Mississippi River Journal*.

"Towards the Sound of a Heron Stepping on Ice": Peter Kurth's *Isadora* provided me with some of the facts concerning the deaths of Isadora Duncan's children; for information on doctored photographs in Stalin's Russia, I made use of David King's *The Commissar Vanishes;* for the details regarding Eadweard Muybridge's murder of Harry Larkyns, I am grateful for Rebecca Solnit's *River of Shadows*.

ACKNOWLEDGMENTS

Some of these poems, sometimes in different versions, previously appeared in the following publications: *Agni:* "Charlie Chaplin Dug Up & Ransomed: A Prayer," "Fumbling with a Field Guide on the Back Arroyo Trail," "Patio Lull with House Guest and View," "*Saint Catherine in an O:* A Song About Knives," "The Scabbard of Limbs Means Flesh," "Second Pilgrimage, Rodeo Nites," "Thumb Trick." *Ashville Poetry Review:* "A Blues About Wanting in the End." *Bellingham Review:* "The Keeper of Hands." *Columbia:* "Portrait of the Whirlwind in Job as a Passenger Pigeon Flock." *Crab Orchard Review:* "Trenton, a Solmization, Two Rivers, a Few Tells." *Ekphrasis:* "A Damaged Fresco of *The Massacre of the Innocents.*" *Gettysburg Review:* "*Night Train:* A Listener's Guide." *Green Mountain Review:* "A Partial Invocation of Our Days," "Pulling Down the Sky." *Kenyon Review:* "Audubon Diptych." *Ontario Review:* "Montezuma's Painters," "Swallowed Things." *Poetry:* "Line," "Shapes of Stone & Prayer."

I am enormously grateful to the National Endowment for the Arts, the W. K. Rose Fellowship, and the New York Times Foundation for enabling me to complete this book.

Many thanks to the editors of the journals where these poems, and others, have appeared. Thanks to Liz Lee, Meg Lemke, and everyone at Houghton Mifflin.

I am deeply indebted to a number of people for their indispensable suggestions, close readings, teachings, and encouragement. Thanks especially to my parents, to my teachers and friends at NYU, to William Appling, Ciaran Berry, Michael Collier, Beth Darlington, Tom Davis, Greg Glazner, Eamon Grennan, Melissa Hammerle, Dana Levin, Phillis Levin, Bob Merce, John Shaw, Tom Sleigh, and Ken Weedin. These poems also owe an incalculable debt to Kathy Graber; I can't imagine what shape this book would have taken without her incisive feedback on line after line.

Profound thanks to Mark Doty for choosing this book and for all of his careful considerations.

Above all, endless thanks to Ligia Bouton, for this shared wonder, for everything. This book would not have been possible without her.

Bread Loaf and the Bakeless Prizes

The Katharine Bakeless Nason Literary Publication Prizes were established in 1995 to expand the Bread Loaf Writers' Conference's commitment to the support of emerging writers. Endowed by the LZ Francis Foundation, the prizes commemorate Middlebury College patron Katharine Bakeless Nason and launch the publication career of a poet, a fiction writer, and a creative-nonfiction writer annually. Winning manuscripts are chosen in an open national competition by a distinguished judge in each genre. Winners are published by Houghton Mifflin Company in Mariner paperback original.

2006 Judges

Mark Doty, poetry
Lan Samantha Chang, fiction
Susan Orlean, creative nonfiction